"It's the story that makes the author, not the other way around."

FORWARD

Fifteen years, a tough transition home from the war in Iraq and a bitter custody battle that left me just 17% of parenting time with my daughter Grace, from a bias and corrupt Nebraska court system is what developed this beautiful curse. Or, did I always just have it? Some may call it narcissism, some may see it as drive, passion or motivation, but whichever you choose to look at it, it's all the same to me. Narcissists, however, always get a bad reputation. We see it all the time, often times with Females posting about how they dated or married a narcissist and how it destroyed them. (Right after they posted their 20th selfie of the day. A narcissist trait of its own). What isn't admitted though, is that it was that narcissists personality that attracted them to that person in the first place. Why? Because a narcissistic personality disorder is described as someone with an inflated sense of self-importance. Proud, confident and attractive. I have been titled as a narcissist and I'm proud of that. My accomplishments and society have instilled this trait in me.

Society though, has also damaged me. It has allowed me to believe that although we have choices in life, we have no control over what happens with those choices. We are not all created equal. We do not all have the same abilities, drive, passions or will to succeed. Some of us are born privileged, destined to succeed and be wealthy, while Others are born without ever living the life of comfort or achievement. They may often times spend their whole lives coming up with ideas of grandeurs while trying to implement them, just to have life remind them that success is not part of the plan. Our book is already written. Simple as that. I also believe however, that life has tolerance for strong people. If we continue to fight for success, eventually life may finally give in to your will to succeed. Not in a year or five years but in my case, fifteen.

Over the last fifteen years, I have developed the need for achievement, competition and leadership. From standing in cages competing in MMA, powerlifting championships, leading thousands on a crusade lobbying the legislature for a shared parenting bill (No bill was passed, but the supreme court acknowledged Nebraska as now a state that doesn't favor, NOR disfavors joint custody). Physique championships, graduating with a bachelor's degree with a learning disability, lobbying the legislature to lower the child support percentages (Accomplished in 2020). Writing and producing documentaries, starting a nonprofit foundation serving military veterans transitioning back into civilian life, to starting a successful law foundation without a law degree. It's easy to see I have a serious addiction for success. I also won a state wrestling championship before the military so, have I always had this trait? Or do I blame it on society or the military? One of the focuses for an upcoming documentary I am writing aims to answer this very question.

Wherever it came from; I call this addiction to achievement "The Beautiful Curse." A beautiful curse is often times just the thoughtfulness of regret. We may have regrets, but we know we can't take anything back. Instead, those regrets we keep inside influence us to remember and act accordingly going forward. Like an internal piece of advice.

In 2020, I embarked on what may be my biggest and toughest goal. To create a documentary series seeking to find the reasons why some veterans find success after service, and why some don't. Why some choose to commit suicide, and why some never even contemplate that option. As I looked deeper into this issue, I began to develop opinions about society, civilians and veterans as a whole rather than groups. Whether or not veterans and civilians should be categorized differently, or if they are actually just one group together as it relates to the suicide epidemics in America. This came to my mind remembering a piece I wrote the day after Philip Seymour Hoffman passed away.

We see it all too often nowadays. Brilliant minds lost with celebrities who have it all, but it's no surprise to those who battle depression and are addicted to ceaseless action. I wrote this after the passing of Phillip Seymour Hoffman, and I would later read it to a large group of individuals at a local University in a PTSD awareness conference. As I spent most of the evening in shock mentally mourning the death of Phillip Seymour Hoffman, my mind wandered to the past and the mourning of Kurt Cobain, Layne Staley, Heath ledger, Robin Williams, Chris Cornell, Anthony Bourdain, and those I personally knew and looked up too that were lost the same way. It's very easy for me to admire those people because they were something of talent and success that I strive to have. More troubling is the fact that I have always been obsessed with the reason, the state of mind, the last moments, and thoughts they had before they died, knowing they had so much more to give to people. I suddenly realized why.

I obviously do not know those individuals or how they lived their lives. I am only making an opinion based on what I have personally taken from their death, but I do know this. The need to be successful can be a sickness if you are unable to be content with your status and the endeavors you have accomplished. For many of us, the motto; "Be comfortable being uncomfortable." Has motivated us towards success or for me, the fight as opposed to the flight response. If you have never lived your life by this, then you will never understand the illness. We struggle with this mental war every day.

There is a very rare disorder that forces some to never be happy, never satisfied and addicted to achieving goals. It is such a rare disorder that it only affects maybe 10% of people, and is not even listed in the DSM. Alexithymia is a disorder that makes people crave ceaseless action to avoid visiting haunting thoughts about negative experiences they have experience. I was introduced to Alexithymia while watching my favorite television show "The Sopranos." Dr. Melfi, brought up the subject, asking Tony if he knew why sharks were always in motion? Going on to explain, that this is a condition that affects people with antisocial personalities. If they aren't constantly engaged in activity and receiving requisite stimulation they tend to crash, falling deep into depression and anxiety while facing the emptiness and self-loathing they may have experienced since childhood. It robs them of emotions, and it makes some unable to be in stable relationships. They don't trust and they are always preparing to be hurt. It's a defense mechanism. Slip away before you're the one that ends up getting hurt and with having no emotions, they don't care who they hurt.

When you come home after going nonstop for 16 hours especially after dropping your child off, it is literally like falling into a black hole. The loneliness and the anxiety are unreal. It's only you, your thoughts, your problems, and it hurts. Respect can have some false impressions because it's tough when you are looked at as a great person, but you're dying inside because you're not happy. It seems to strengthen depression because you feel like you haven't really achieved what others believe you are capable of. I have battled this for many years. I believe depression is the devils work. They say when you do good things for people or the world, the devil will put something in your life to punish you for it. I have sometimes wondered if a brilliant mind is punished with depression.

You have the choice to withstand the feelings from the putrid soul which deviates from your brilliance, or you have the choice to find something to take you away from that feeling. For many it's addiction. It comes down to not being able to distinguish between dreams, reality or not having the ability to cope with being alone. It's a disease that will not allow us to be detained to the normal way of life that most know and instinctively except, but it's human nature that fights for that need to feel loved and surrounded. It's an inner and lonely battle that forces the emotions that we hide to rear its bitter face, reminding us that we are alive. For those that experienced stardom at a young age and never truly understood the depths of normalcy, and who spent most of their life experiencing the luxuries that follow popularity; the reality, the aging process and the realization that it's all over, and that the time to do for yourself, which includes finding other talents, for some I think is just too much to face.

We must understand that it's a disease that can only be cured by those effected and not by meds or counseling. The difference between life and death when you are at your lowest point of your story is finding the ambition, and motivation that your time of triumph is ahead. Most cannot fathom the fact that we are at our strongest when we are at rock bottom. I have always believed it is life's test for us to dig deep down inside and find our strengths and talents and use those as our reasons to survive and succeed. In many ways it has saved my life. The only advantage we have in life is staying positive.

With this documentary, I do not expect there to be a simple analogy of any kind. I do not believe we can ever fix what wanders in our minds. We can alter it, but we can't change it indefinitely. What I hope to achieve is a new awareness, and to change the way we look at the issue of success and suicide in order to understand that it really isn't as complex as psychologists and society believes it to be.

Within this book are the confines of some of the most challenging and darkest moments of my life, but within these tribulations are also the words that shadowed some of my greatest accolades as well. We are all just one idea and one day closer to our greatest moments, and part of the therapy in realizing this was writing.

I've never thought about my writings in a way that they could somehow help others, the same way they have helped me. For the longest time I kept these private because I wasn't confident or interested sharing a hobby that was different than the others, I was more known for. As I slowly started sharing my work however, I could see that there were some who understood my poems and were grateful. Whether the appreciation of my work were showcased as tattoos, shared on social media or through a simple text or message, I was honored and humbled for the appreciation. That's when I began to think about completing a book of poems and quotes. Whether they can continue to help others or not, at the very least I now have a haven for my work in this book.

Dedicated to those affected by the demons of depression and the outcome of suicide.

"The true art of writing is not thinking about what you're writing when you're writing, but coming back to it later and understanding where it came from."

Beautifully Cursed

WALLOWED VISIONS

Raindrops fall with the pain that floods my
heart.
I can do without you until you part.
Soul soaked pills fill a bottomless pit,
a pit that has drained what was once a happy
meadow.

You have chosen to instill sacred lies,
lies that I am forced to swallow like lighting
filled skies.
I wallow in my visions.
Visions of retribution like sins hang over the
heads of prisoners.
Though, I am a prisoner.
A prisoner of a mistake that I will never regret.
So, I must stand as fingers point like they've
witnessed a man executed for a wrongful death.

Your heart will never compare.
Compare to mine, you'll see yours has been
unfair.
Not just to me within your desperate pleas,
but to an innocent mind whose eyes you have
kept blind.

PLOW

I am that plow.
Solid, rough and useless unless needed.
Sharp at the edges, shiny and detailed;

I am meant for dirt.
Breaking the ground no one else dare touch.

Though you may have the seeds to plant
progression, growth and change for mankind.
Though you may be the driver, skilled in the
trade;
there is no direction in mind.

My arrowed shape knows the direction.
I welcome those seeds.
I know the process will never be developed
without changing the lay of this ground.

While struggling through this dirt
and remembering that without struggle there
will never be progress,
without the tools to change unstable foundation,
there can never be solid development for a new
horizon.

LOOSE LEAF SORROW

I sleep alone in this bed,
Just as I dream as one in my head.
I walk the side streets where no one else stands,
I sing a song that no one understands.

You're far from this place where I saw you,
but our hearts still live within the same beat.
The same speed as when I first met you.

I say hello, but they don't hear me.
I try to love but it isn't easy.
I am invisible without you since you left.
Time seems to now stand still.
My eyes have no color without your fill.

I haven't been the same since you've been gone.
I'm like the leaves in the fall that just can't hang on.
I keep waiting for a new season so that I can feel that life within me,
but without your rain, I remain asleep.

Your tears fill my heart with sorrow.
So, I'll sleep as we continue to wait for tomorrow.
You're far from this place where I saw you,
but our hearts still live within the same beat.
The same speed as when I met you.

UNPAVED TEARS

The fog never clears, it just dwindles in my vision.
The pain never dulls, it just aches through my pulse.
The anger never hides, it just assaults within my voice.
The regrets never forgive, but rather punishes within every problem.

I have never felt so alone.
I have never hated this much.
I have never tried so hard for a tear.

The sun never shines, it just hides behind the
truth.
The streets are never paved,
but rather crack from every time they are used.
The ground is never fertile,
only dry from lack of necessity.

I have never felt so alone.
I have never hated this much.
I have never tried so hard for a tear.

IMPERMISSABLE FLEEDING'S

Hell is the impossibility of reason.
I need your eyes like I need a new season.
Changes don't come around here like they used
too.
So, I'm destined to stand here and wait for the
truth.
She once asked me on her way to a goodbye;
when she would come before this child?

I'll take those lonely nights remembering that
question.
Hoping that's not all that's out there.

Lawyers are only your friends when you have
money
and judges only care who did who wrong unless
you're the lady.
Seems so hard to stay sane in a world destined
to blame.

Hell is the impossibility of reason.
I need your eyes like I need a new season.
Changes don't come around here like they used
too.
So, I'm destined to stand here and wait for the
truth.
Bottles of cologne I own reflect the past woman
who bought them.
The lashing against my character I received
proved there was no reason.
I'll continue to stand with my book of many
men,
and you can try to read it is as if you know the
outcome in the end.

PEACEFULLNESS

The snow falls slowly, like a comfortable affair.
The wind blows by like a race to get away from
an uncomfortable stare.
The red sky hangs on for as long as I can see.
The moon daunts into the shadows and in its
face reflects me.

It's not the years that fly by, but us that stand
still.
The courage and the passion we cannot build.
We are too afraid to jump into the beautiful
dance.
Often regretting the day, we never took a
chance.

The water is still like glass.
Desperately waiting for a drop of rain to make
it dance.
The trees shake with the breeze, echoing
throughout the days.
The mellow happiness within their leaves.

A baby coos in a room, never knowing the
pains the years will bring.
An old man lies dying, waiting for the day all
that pain goes away.

It's the peacefulness in things we cannot feel
that inside us, we must instill.
If only for one small moment where everything
seems right.

THE RAIN

For months I've lived like the dirt.
The ground I have become has been
without the rain.
My heart takes each drop vigorously

and soaks the need before I can get a taste.

For days my tongue has been dry.
I have spit nothing but the anger for the
need too.
Clouds have casted shadows over my hopes;
leaving nothing but the vision of a day turned
blue.
Lightning has shown its strength,
but dealt nothing but compassion for its
consequences.

Winds have shown its force,
but left nothing to respect the circumstances.
Another sunrise will come to show its warmth,
and another sunset will veer its victory over our
lives,
but without the rain a part of us dies.

THE MIRROR

There sometimes comes a time in an old man's
life when he looks in the mirror.
Really, looks into the mirror.
Past the stubbles and the wrinkles,
but into the face.
Deep into the face.

He remembers times that were good;
the stages, the staggers and how he rose up.
He acknowledges triumphs, uproars,

the victories that cost him blood
and why he's a legend.

He then looks into his eyes.
Deep into his eyes,

realizing those staggers only lasted a minute,
that he never actually stayed up;
those triumphs never celebrated meaning,
those victories never made him a legend
and that blood was spilled rather than shed.

The mirror is more than just a reflection of you.
It's a reflection of where you've been,
what you've become and who you are as a
person.
Make sure your life has meaning,
the hands you were blessed with touch hope;
the battles you choose equal victory
and the blood you shed drenches truth.
So, that someday when you face that mirror you
won't be ashamed of who you are.

COUNTRY ROAD STRANDS

Theses country roads seem to etch the strands
in my brain.
Each stretch points to a place I recall along
memory lane.
Good friends and good times seem far, but near
in my heart.

Every ending leads right back to the start.

Tonight, I said goodbye to my past good times
and my last early party on the way to sunup.
No more last hurrahs or long applauses.
I've said goodbye to the legendary status that
never really was.

No more conversations about the past.
No one wants to buy me a beer.
No reason to be early because everyone wants
to arrive last.
The thickness of the party now feels thin.
Everyone has filled their time.
Most have fallen in love and moved down the
line.

Youth is gone and what a ride it was.
I'm now just a man that looks kind of familiar.
A name one may think they heard of over the
years.

THE BOTTOM

So, this is what the bottom feels like?
When you've been reaching out to others,
but the hands don't trade favors.
When a has been was something,
then feels the pain of nothing.

When you're a qualified fixture, but not good
enough for the role.
When the women come in multitudes, but you
just can't love.
When desires starving, but you just can't feed it.

So, this is what the bottom feels like?
Scraping the floor for an ounce of hope?
This is what the bottom feels like;
pleading with the last inch of rope.

So, this is what the bottom feels like?
Selling everything you own to anyone that has a
home?
Asking god to protect you from the bills instead
of the hand that kills?
Having to fight in order to keep your child.
Trained to hide emotion because the cause of
them will break you.
When desires starving, but you just can't feed it.

So, this is what the bottom feels like?
Scraping the floor for an ounce of hope?
This is what the bottom feels like;
pleading with the last inch of rope.

When the pain of regret can't seem to beat the
pride.
Wondering if the dirt on your hands is worth
those that died.
When the heat that comforts your home isn't
worth the payment.

When a possibility looks to you, but you don't know how to lead it.
When sleep is your escape from pain, but you just can't afford it.
When desires starving, but you just can't feed it.

So, this is what the bottom feels like?
Scraping the floor for an ounce of hope?
This is what the bottom feels like.
Pleading with the last inch of rope.

COMFORTABLE

I just want to be comfortable.
I want to sustain the person that I am.
I want to look in the mirror and recognize the face.
I want to stand on the ground and know it's fertile.
I want to tell someone who I am and not have to ramble.

I just want to be comfortable.
I want to know that what I put in; I get out.
I want to go to sleep and be sure of what I've done that day.
I want to wake up with an agenda that's less than the sunset.
I want to finish my day knowing I have a home.
I want a check that's more than what I owe.

I just want to be comfortable.
I want a conversation with people
and not have to wonder where I've seen them.
I want to enjoy the time with my child
and not worry about how limited it is.
I want my mind to set itself on idle.
For once, I'd like to be on the same page as life
and not fear the next chapter.

I just want to be comfortable.
I want to lie next to someone
and not have to wonder how long it will last.
I want to take love up on its offer and be totally
committed.
I want to know the beat of my heart is in
cadence with another.

I just want to be comfortable.
I want to be ok with average,
relax, and feel inner warmth of things unseen.
When sadness occurs, I want to shed a tear.
I want to know what I stand for really stands for
something.

I just want to be comfortable.
I want to know the battles I've endured made a
difference.
I want to know the strides I've made helped
someone.
When my days are numbered and the time is
slow, I just want to be comfortable.

When life flashes before me and the nights are
my penance;
when the sun rises, and I'm given forgiveness;
when I see my kin grown and what my fight
meant for her,
I want to be comfortable.

When my shadows fade, when that bright light
zeros in on me
and what purpose in life I made;
I can be comfortable.

SUMMER SNOW

The May snow fall flirts through the summer
skies;
like a meaningful question slides through your
thin disguise.
I don't recognize this season, and I don't
understand those eyes.
If you thought you were out of options, couldn't
you see me there?
You built a wall around you, so my words were
unclear.
Were you too weak to endure what it took?
Did you think you could escape being a
woman?
Were you trying to hide from your mistakes?

You choose to comfort yourself in pain.
You had a lie for every day.

A simple smile to develop truth.
My ignorance I never knew.
If you thought you were out of options,
couldn't you see me there?
You built a wall around you
so, my words were unclear.
Were you too weak to endure what it took?
Did you think you could escape being a
woman?
Were you trying to hide from your mistakes?

Now this child we are feeding has many
tongues.
You try and convince yourself there's only one.
The love in her eyes will never fade,
and my fight to see them will only remain.
Your days of being naive are ending.
When will you stop pretending?

Efforts continue to question my integrity.
Who's feeding your addiction?
Can't you see you're feeding my addiction?
The memory of the saddest day of my life
will forever overshadow the happiness.
How you chose that day to show the real you.

If you thought you were out of options,
couldn't you see me there?
You built a wall around you
So, my words were unclear.
Were you too weak to endure what it took?

Did you think you could escape being a
woman?
Were you trying to hide from your mistakes?

MOONLIGHT DASH

The power in that full moon reminds me;
I bet being in love is just as great.
Time means nothing anymore.
Every day is the same dream in repeat.
Those black clouds seem to cover over it
and the fact that the moon is powerful;
just the way our fears cover our hearts
and what's right in moral.

We remain for eternity in debt to what we could
have been.
Rather than what options are awkwardly staring
at us now and again.
We want to blame our mothers and the system
for our imperfections
just like we want to blame that DVR for
keeping us from helping the worlds addictions.

Karma is about as good as that occasional
sickness.
We are all owed it.
We can reflect from it or call it getting even,
but the medications are the same.
Wars will always be our culture.
Its face and dangers are different,

but we are all fighting one right now.
We are all veterans.

The biggest insult to the life you were given
is simply never helping anyone but yourself.
There are two dates in time that define us;
everyone knows what they mean.
What's important is the time that was known in
that little dash in between.

TIMELESS TRAGEDIES

One day from wasting my time, again. Again.

Now I got questions about my answers. Defend.

Simplicity at its finest is now complicated.
Amends.

Fighting for my rights has myself defeated.
Regrets.

Respect in all nature always changes shades.
The same way different colors always blossom
beautifully in flowers. Timelessly.

You're Like a beautiful flower that somehow
grows through the rocks of a mountain; you're
like a beautiful something. Remembrance.

Love in retrospect will always trade for
loneliness. Comforting.

Mind games at best will always fill a void.
Heartless.

Desire defeating laziness amounts to well-
being. Repeating.

Intention always defeats laziness. Action.

Friendships consist of convenience. Betrayal.

Bulging veins and sunken cheeks always means
experience. Life.

An offering hand never trades hands. Guilty.
Respect in all nature always changes shades,
the same way different colors always blossom
beautifully in flowers. Timelessly.

You're Like a beautiful flower that somehow
grows through the rocks of a mountain.
You're like a beautiful something.
Remembrance.

BORED

Tonight, I have finally given in to a life of
boredom.
I have retired and stopped all calls for freedom.
I put a detour sign in front of memory lane,

and refuse to let the adrenaline from an old
song flow through my veins.

Has understood the reason people settle down
with one another.
Excepted some were never friends and others
were just lovers.
Come to realize being bored is much like being
an addict.
You crave excitement and will do anything to
get it.

I see the investment with the raising of
children.
I feel the loneliness of seeing them like old
friends.
Boredom keeps those around who once brought
us that fire,
but now that the flame is out, so should that
desire.

If I show no devotion and get none in return,
it's time to walk away.
There's plenty of bridges to burn.

MY SWEET FRIEND DESTINY

The only person who ever equaled me in
pointless passion.
Sometimes living too many dreams becomes
the end to one's life story.

Like spending too much time proving others wrong,
takes the meaning out of glory.

When caring too much for others takes concern away from yourself,
you're trying too hard and will never be satisfied.
Sometimes appreciation for others never allows you to be respected.
You hate so much, you become immune to love and affection.

When all you do is wrong, nothing else seems right.
Just like Lessons learned from experiences takes away from life.
Sometimes every effort failed outlines every other creation,
and success created brilliantly alters motivated temptation.

When love comes too easy and lust consumes us like tragedy,
trying to find the truth in aggression always equals vulnerability.
When all you do is dream, there is no room for reality.
When reality comes intact, there's no longer passion for the ability.

BACKROAD TO NOWHERE

This feeble-minded emptiness reflects tasks
undone.
These Nebraska back roads all look the same,
like songs unsung.
We know these songs so intimately, but can't
seem to sing in tune
Like words unspoken that never seemed more
true.

Time has never paid the effort it put forth,
and our dreams reflect grasps slipped with
regrets soaked in remorse.
We lie in our sleep convulsing with missed
opportunities,
because we never inhaled the futures
possibilities.

Eyes cry for needs unprecedented.
Our hearts lead onward to tales of stories gone
and misprinted.
Unmarked graves lie of legends unknown;
proved all along those battles were fought
alone.

Silence masks souls undaunted, though pulses
felt, beats not confronted.
Electricity between bodies have never been
ignited,
and loss of life have never been righted.

One ounce of adrenaline inflicts the will to
succeed;
the meaning of life and the addiction of need.

FLOODED FOG

You're like the flood that fills my eyes,
when I can't control when emotion starts.
No matter how I try to restrain the feelings,
your love fills this heart.

Nobody knows me, not even me.
Like not knowing the forest when you're the
trees.
You're the sunlight that shines to the greens,
and you're the rain that feeds these leaves.

When the night turns dim, and it's just me and
him;
I think of your skin and I'm all in.
The taste of your lips is the forbidden fruit.
The perspiration in your passion, I inject every
drip.

You don't know lonely until you face this life
alone.
Until this pulse has no blood to feed that soul.
It makes no difference where I turn,
when that flame still burns.
I keep telling myself I'll see past that fog, and I
will learn.

You're like the flood that fills my eyes,
when I can't control when emotion starts.
No matter how I try to restrain the feelings,
your love fills this heart.
Though that sun doesn't shine on me anymore;
I feel no heat, and I'll purge for more.

I'll keep searching for that feeling that was
gone with you.

CONTROL

I won't let the night take my focus.
I won't let criminals evoke my past.
I won't let trials erupt my fears.
I'll wrap my fists so their built to last.

I won't let judges determine my role.
I won't let history sculpt my future.
I won't let war placate victory.
I'll take another blow in becoming a fixture.

I won't let my sorrows determine my pain.
I won't let loneliness control emotion.
I won't let failure constitute loss.
I'll take another step with plans in motion.

I won't let kings demand my beliefs.
I won't let the battle wear me down.
I won't let scriptures control my passion.

I'll use my stamina and take their crown.

I'll take my ideas and turn them into gold.
I'll prepare for this mission despite defeat.
I'll use this frustration to transform conflict.
I'll take this love and make it legendary.

TEARS FOR TEARS

The words we need in life are too expensive to
search for, but it's those that we need to trigger
the soul.
A tear is a tear, but they all fall differently.
It's what signifies the meaning that constitutes
its weight.
The speed that is surpassed equals the feeling
and it's the decision that's made that reminds us
of the lesson.

Uncompromised ways equal hidden hurt.
It's a shame we don't see the true damage in
indecision.
Feelings not seen often result in pain,
but who are we supporting?
Ourselves or the ones we love?

Hatred leads our swords.
We stab what we are unsure of,
and we run from shadows that are our own.
When the sun sets and it's the same shade of
dark,

it's too late to see the shadows were nothing,
but an Illusion.
We have nothing left, but the sun to set on the
truth.
Nowhere to hide, no reason to blame.
Only the masses see the realism.

The thunder sets in on the appeal of corruption.
Everyone has shelter, but you.
The rain reigns down and you have no
protection.
No excuse for the fact that your decision left
you vulnerable.
You have no guidance to safety,
and you have no bible for direction.
No plans for another excuse.
No way to turn back time.

The times of before will surpass the future of
legacy.
What you said, and what you stood for;
the demise you promised you fought against.
The tears you looked back on doesn't amount to
the ones the drive produce.
The saddest tears cause you to realize,
the years of the past are behind you.

Those with you all along are now gone.
It's just you, the wheel, the intoxicants and the
memories.
There's nothing more tearful than the
realizations you've been alone forever,

and there's nothing more factual than the historic truth in self-reliance.

Wasted time results in progress of the unexpected protected.
We have always been alone, and alone we die with regrets.
The words we lived by, and what we searched for are now left to trigger the soul.
Tears for tears.
It's what signifies the meaning that constitutes what's left of our legacy.

THE DELUSIONAL BEING

You're not who you claim to be when you are surrounded and subjected.
Laughing and smiling while really your crying deep inside.
You're not as powerful as your projected.

That sweet taste of liqueur escapes reality into belligerence.
You talk about anything to anyone who will listen because they're all liars too,
and they'll toast to your ignorance.

You tell each other you've loved beauty queens, but really your fearsome of rejections.
You're all addicted to whores with fake breasts and fake personalities.

They're easy to comfort your needs.

You say you got money and a nice car,
but nothing to prove they're yours.
None of your friends ask
because their afraid their lies are longer than
yours.

You say you're busy,
you have agendas, a schedule and a goal.
Girl, you've never helped nobody but yourself,
and never been on time for charity that isn't
your own.

You claim to be successful,
but your bullshit is more impressive.
You talk about struggle and pain,
but I crush you with just a stare.

Your tattoos are intimidating to your trust fund
buddies,
but my scars outline a life you could never
handle.
You made it through college you say,
but I've forgotten more then you'll ever know.
You don't even know yourself.

There's poison in that dance
and the days are growing thin.
Then, it's just you and him.
Reality from within.

SHELTERED WIND

Take shelter from this marvelous rain.
Withstand pressure from the winds of change.
Deny the lightening in that frightening feature.
Pick up the wreckage from the daunting floods
in your future.
You tell yourself you have possessions you're
worried about.
I got nothing, so I smile.
Waiting for the damage so you can understand
the pain I've had for a while.

You sink with every inch of rain.
You fall farther from reality with every gust of
wind.
Unknowing life's already left you with every
regret from within.
So, press your worries against that glass,
and wait for the storm to pass.
Remember your dreams, because they never
last.

Hold on to that new love that forms.
Remember mistakes that you never learned
from and carry that storm.
Pull yourself from that cover because the mud
only sinks you.
The lighting may crash, but you'll pull through.
The rain can't soak what is not there
because Passion will float above any flood.

Luxuries will never compare to love unknown.
So, hold on to that new love that forms.
Remember mistakes that you never learned
from and carry that storm.

DESIRE TO POSSESS

I collect beautiful smiles while I where a frown.
I pretend I'm lost when I'm in my own town.
I want to travel fast, but I take the back roads.
I want to be someone else, so I put on another's
clothes.

I want to shake hands properly, but my grips
too loose.
I tried to love once, but I had too much to lose.
I would like to take communion, but I don't like
the taste.
I would like to settle down, but there's too
much time to waste.
I want to feel the warmth of the sun, but the
sweats too much to take.
I want to be proud of my job, but it depends
how much I make.

I want to escape this rain, but I enjoy the
sadness.
I want a normal life, but I thrive on its madness.
I want to rid these addictions, but they're my
only friends.

I want to say I'm sorry, but I can't seem to make
amends.
I want to find reasons to worship, but I'm
enabled by hardship.
I want to bring down this wall, but I'm only
strong enough to crawl.

I want to find the devotion in trust, but the
gamble is too much.
I want to be inflicted with love and attention,
but there's nothing more hypocritical and
conflicted.
I want to be on the outside looking in, but I'm
still numb from within.
I want to be inside looking out, but I'm scared
to know what reality's about.
I want to remain the same because it's easier to
live with blame.
I want to remain the same because it's easier to
live for blame.

WHY
("Vallum Poetry Magazine" Submission)

We sit on these benches and watch the cars go
by,
we want to be the drivers; we want another life.
Why the driver?
Why not the journey?
Strangers pass by like fairy tales in a story.
We want to be the character; we want the glory.

Why the fairy tale?
Why the character?
Why not the creator?
Why life?
Why a driver?
Why not the journey?

We lay silently as a plane flies by, like a distant memory.
We imagine the destination; we want to be free.

Why the memory?
Why the destination?
Why not the pilot?
Why the fairy tale?
Why the character?
Why not the creator?
Why life?
Why a driver?
Why not the journey?

Ships sail toward the end of the world, like dreams we continue to let fade.
We wonder what's over that edge, we want to escape.

Why the dreams?
Why the end?
Why not the ocean?
Why the memory?
Why the destination?
Why not the pilot?

Why the fairy tale?
Why the character?
Why not the creator?
Why life?
Why a driver?
Why not the journey?

We stare at the dancing wheat fields like ideas
that come and go,
imagining the feeling in the flow.
We want to be at peace.

Why ideas?
Why feelings?
Why not the wind?
Why the dreams?
Why the end?
Why not the ocean?
Why the memory?
Why the destination?
Why not the pilot?
Why the fairy tale?
Why the character?
Why not the creator?
Why life?
Why a driver?
Why not the journey?

Staring at the lights of the ambulance like
sudden déjà vu.
Wondering about the casualty, we are
OBSESSED with tragedy.

Why Déjà vu?
Why tragedy?
Why not the lesson?
Why ideas?
Why feelings?
Why not the wind?
Why the dreams?
Why the end?
Why not the ocean?
Why the memory?
Why the destination?
Why not the pilot?
Why the fairy tale?
Why the character?
Why not the creator?
Why life?
Why a driver?
Why not the journey?

Let the journey carry you to travels entrenched.
Creators are born within life's memories
clenched.
Pilot's destinations are not always formally
planned.
The oceans waves control all motivation within
man.
The winds will carry you to places chapters lie.
Lessons form when it threatens life.

CRUCIFIED HUMILITY

Today, I lost all judgement for sinners.
I know that battle from within evokes no
winners.
Calmly emerging in guilty pleasures;
the good deeds failed brings no measures.

When your thoughts become your biggest fear,
it's only because there's nobody there to lend an
ear.
Repeated pictures fill your mind.
That cold dark room looms while you try and
unwind.
Convulsing with Prayers for the struggle that
awaits you tomorrow
You fade away to sleep in the comfort of
sorrow.

I continue to inhale humidity.
I exhale bitter chills that blind you
committedly.
Will burning my candle at both ends, ignite the
middle and explodes into virtue?
Have you felt the adrenaline of hunger and
given blood for fuel?

My eyes have never felt so heavy, hoping the
twitching doesn't mean the end.
These Fever dreams are just like living my own
life.
Eventually, I'll mend.

I'm a survivor.
In the books I live life subconsciously.
Suicide isn't a way to escape life,
it's a way to survive unconsciously.

This loneliness and boredom are too much to
take.
These nights are quiet and missing my child, I
can't shake.
Crucified for sins undone, to be a father to a
son.

BELONGING

I just don't belong.
Like a sunny day in a storm,
or a daisy in a pasture of wheat.
As Beautiful people don't mingle for long,
it's not wrong to feel threatened by beauty.

Beauty is often found in the ugliest of souls.
Like rainbows can appear from a torrential
storm.
Minds are the most hypocritical blessings, like
brilliant ideas.
People want to think about it,
dream about it and complain about it,
but not be about it.

There has come a time when there are no longer
friends.
Friends are now the wind.
The sounds of leaves ruffling, our only
memories.
It's a wonder we become loners in life.

As the rains that bring nurturing for bloom,
the fall takes the reward, then nothing to use.
I understand through my insanity the
temptations to be free.
Like the comatose still rely on sound, and the
lame to be.
Winters are boredom,
like moments just after sunset.

Grave reminders and recollections daunt the
Deering from the last shades of day.
It's impressive how we can crave a place never
seen,
remembering the same feeling when Some
chose death over progression.

Memories outweigh growth,
the future and some who can't fathom age.
I'm a soldier paying the price because I
survived.
Quivers reject the turning of a page.
Can you really tell the difference between a
smile and pain?
Can you differ from the sun and rain?

LOVE

(Resulted in a tattooed quote from a fan)

Love is interests that will never leave,
like the first time you hear your new favorite
song.
Endless, timeless and you'll always sing along.

Love is your favorite book.
Where the words never change,
the beginning is known,
parts remembered, but still exciting.
Though you know how it ends, you know it
ends in happiness.

Love Is the sunrise.
It's always there and always will be.
Even through the darkest days.
Reminders that yesterday is gone and will be
again.
Positive in its future.

Love is the sunset, and the comfort in its time.
The way it sets, the beauty in its familiarity, the
vision of it never fades,
and although it disappears, you know it ends
the same tomorrow.

Love is the first intimate encounter.
Nervousness in touch and unfamiliar.

Uncomfortable with feeling and dumb.
The memory of lust is addicting.

Love is generated from pain and struggle.
Never enjoyed with feelings of comfort.
Instead, garnished from the passion to survive
the tides of failure and loss.

Love is protection, not perfection.
Love is failure, nothing secure.
Love is defeat, not triumph.
Love is hate, not trust.
Love is memory, not the future.
Love Is loss, not discovery.
Love is a broken heart, not trust.

It's what erupts within our souls that create the
true emotions in love.
The pain in regret and the loss of something
sacred to instill what really matters.
Something that can create a memory to carry us
through the hard times.
It's what can never be lost in passion that gives
us reason to love.

PEPPERCORN HEARTBEAT

I look upon the fields and catch the orange
glow of a far-off sunset through the leafless
branches.
I'm alone, though I've always been alone.

Just me and my sick passion to be above
average.

The sun reaches around the corner just enough
to tap me on the shoulder,
reminding me that brighter days are ahead.
I'm guilty of who I am, in a place where there's
no amends.
I need a break inside your smile, so I'm
reminded of friends.

I love waking to the sound of rain, the clouds,
and the darkness take away the pain.
I'm alive somewhere I swear.
A solid being does fill the clothes I wear.
Like a peppercorn heartbeat, I do exist.
Though only through the vision of an
ultrasounds mist.

I tasted love once but didn't react to the texture.
I figured the buffet was better.
Now I'm bulimic.
The end of certain triumphs has exhausted.
Owe a lot to lawyers, owed a lot to friends, but
never have they traded hands.

I believed the fight was worth risking my life.
The dead were unlucky, and I was unscathed.
What it was worth I'll never know.
The safe place I envisioned only makes me
want to go back though.

I encompass love with addiction, though my
thirst is love, and attention.
I live alone and buried in a forest covered
haven.
No one knows it's just me, my dreams and my
past.

Like a peppercorn heartbeat I do exist.
Though only through the vision of an
ultrasounds mist.
I tasted love once but didn't react to the texture.
I figured the buffet was better, and now I'm
bulimic.
The end of certain triumphs has exhausted.
Owe a lot to lawyers, owed a lot to friends but
never have they traded hands.

Like a peppercorn heartbeat I do exist.
Though only through the vision of an
ultrasounds mist.
I tasted love once but didn't react to the texture.
I figured the buffet was better, and now I'm
bulimic.
The end of certain triumphs has exhausted.
Owe a lot to lawyers, owed a lot to friends but
never have they traded hands.

SUN DRAPED CASKETS

Show me a hero and I'll build you a tragedy.
Men never die without a legacy.

Sun draped caskets and tombstones portray a meaning to life,
but there's never been a remembrance or visit from the moonlight.

Soul soaked mornings are often monumental.
Something about the dawn brings penance to something beautiful.
Always dreaming but never dreamed of.
Like flowers noticed, but never picked upon.

Ideas of wonderful creations,
but never the motivation to build from frustrations.
Ripples along the banks give reminders of gratitude, motions of earth and the reflection of livelihood.

Snowflakes inflict the tongue long enough to remind you another season is near.
Winds reflect the past, and what your presence has meant the last year.
Thoughts must presume other's diseases to nurture your own.
So that the miracles of healing will result in healing on your own.

Little breaths of babies remind you of innocence,
as the rest of your life results in impotence.
We gather in masses to change aggression.
While we turn around and give our opponents attention.
Like awaking to the sun not seen in months;
feeling the warmth, then squinting from its front.
Show me a tragedy and I'll find you the hero.
Thought and regret that shouldn't have resulted in zero

Trials and war have created my appearance.
There's a triumph in every word.
The results from my passions in life have built my legacy.
Remembering anger should be developed into something beautiful.
Not something destructive.

UNTITTLED

The passing of summer is like the passing of youth.
All the things we never got around to doing saddens the soul and resembles regret.

Regrets overshadow the progress that builds
character, confidence is flirtation and love
means any form of instant gratification.

The beginning of fall signifies the end of time.
The smell of mildew resembles a place
remembered.
No more is there a forever
because self-confidence has become narcissism.

Truth is retired like the meaning of loyalty.

The moon shines a resentful glow
onto the fact that reality is my biggest fear.
The diagnosis of a brilliant mind discovers the
disease of talent.
Every passion that reigns from our legacy is
one more reason for our sickness.

The greatest sadness from within, are the
expectations of people.
When every day you wake up and ask yourself
if it's worth it;
expecting others to help themselves.

I hear them talk, and I see disillusion.
I hear complaints, and I see their anger.
They are broke, but I see no confidence.
I ask for their passion but receive open hands.

The greatest investment is fear.
It's the only way we know we are alive.

We love when you're fighting for your legacy,
its purpose, and we smile when you give up.

There is no remorse for the weak.

MEANINGFUL COLLATERAL

Minds right but passions tangled.
A concoction to something tragic.
Thoughts can only feed from each other
until the ideas erode.

The night and its spin on the day ahead,
makes the future amazing.
As the rain beads perfectly down the leaves,
its pure residue suits inner simplicity.

Remembering the times my fingers ran silently
through the silk of your cheeks.
I can't find a memory worth reliving,
and I can't remember kindness that wasn't
worth giving.

How the sorrows bring the times we never
embraced.
Reminds me the laughter from my child is the
meaning of innocence.
The first time I felt those lips is still the greatest
investment.
The first time I forgot the reward brought my
greatest defeat.

Tasks undone become a song unsung.
We take that first step but realize the dangers in
the trek.
Her spontaneous movements in her pleasures,
resemble the perfect fixtures in a pretty picture.

The way of life that you never saw fit,
pertains to the norms you created from within.
A stranger that draws your attention
sometimes signals a need for affection.

Her face often seemed blank,
and I loved the way it would make me think.
The thoughts of what made a person sad,
connects to your own worries of what drives
you mad.

A beautiful day can suddenly bring the rain.
As you bring the people laughter,
you go home and medicate from pain.
There is no meaning thereafter.

The favorite part of my days
was the way she said, "I love you."
The happiness I feel now is that memory,
 but not the clue.

Absence grows founder, like winds cooling a
wound.
Deep with impressions, like feeling the speed of
my heartbeat for you.

Life never reflects a moment that wasn't
nurtured into growth.
Time remembers regrets indebted to the rest of
your life.

PEACEFUL PLEASURES

Time has certainly passed me by,
but your love keeps me active and alive.
Your love is the rain.
It produces the growth of the soul and keeps me
captive in life.
Though I am not the plants, I reign as chivalry
in nature.
I soak every drop of moisture, so I don't
become a creature.

Though, I never soaked in enough.

Never has a high wind ever felt so calm and
real when I'm with you.
The ripples in the sea creates every emotion I
feel, and I know it's true.
It's timeless, like the memories you've created
in my mind.
Without the thought of more, part of me dies.

My eyes lose themselves as they cast into
yours.
Like staring through a set of trees,
there's a patch of land perfect for seclusion,
need, and it's comforting.

When the sun is settling in on another forgotten
dream;
visions sustain the promises of tomorrow, and
in it will still be you and me.
When I view deep into your insights of
pleasure,
my heart and my pulse beat with leisure, and
it's pleasing.

Flickering lights of a lonely passing train
through the flurries,
offers a last penance to the season and reason
not to worry.
A slow rumble of a peaceful and haunting
storm creeps alongside the hills.
Although I'm frightened, I know you will heal
my fears, and I'm at peace.

As I think of reasons why certain stars never
fall from the sky,
and others fall with their last triumph for a
reason why;

I begin to think about all the love I have for a
friend.
I would give anything to relive those feelings
with you again and it's amazing.

The question that shall take you to the center of
the universe is simple, and indebted.
How many sunsets have you seen that you
regretted?
How many sunrises have you really waited for?
Alongside you, is their room for more?

You can control everything from anything
inside of passion.

CHARISMATIC BRIGADE

Virtue finds itself in depressions realms.
Failure has no friends, and dust creates the
amends.
With no cross to bear, I shake what demon's
terror.
Addictions have no cure when the pains still
there.
I'll follow you down to the wicked garden,
where you laid to rest.

Where your charismatic dances pertained to a
brilliant minds brigade.
With a lost soul, sleep is temptation because the
frustrations lie.
Your dreams are for sale, but the scam no one
will buy.

Your soul is a shell from what it used to be.
Denial is the pulse that inflicts your heartbeat.
I'll follow you down to the wicked garden,
where you laid to rest.
Where your charismatic dances pertained to a
brilliant minds brigade.

WINTER CHILL

This December rain is haunting.
Like a sad season that just won't end.
The creaking of an old wood floor is daunting.
A reminder of how old life really is.

Ghosts will always haunt antique houses.
Like legends that exist through the fog;
they will always hear voices
when walking through the fields alone.

Lies and trust are not always in you.
Inside I create movies when I'm feeling
glamorous.

It's the easiest way to hide the truth.
Pretending we are someone else is contagious.

Victories in wars and rings are born from pain.
Just the way the seas were tortured,
from the rivers that emptied the floods
from torrential rains.

Just as the fields of feathers seem to comfort.
The winds arise from storms that move the
earth.
I'm a creator and I'm a dreamer of support.
Passive.
I give ideas birth.

Loneliness erodes the structure of being.
Addicted to possibilities of attraction,
my genetics in lust have cheated love, and what
it means.
Love Conflicts the outcomes of reaction.

I'm a walking failure through dreams,
and I'm hiding from my own home.
A place through pain in a world close to means
I'll always be respected here alone.

There she sits, creating that cigarette smoke.
I sit here watching the beauty with the lights
low.
I imagine her feeling while letting this drink
flow.

We never notice the contractual beauty until it
goes.

The saddest days ahead lie within the rest of my
life.
Watching my child grow without my presence;
confused, unsure and without the definition of
strife.

Within those tragedies of life, I have lived
through the harm that is being done.
May our children learn to give
when kindness is given, and then undone.

For we all endure sadness, pain and regret.
We will always sin as a result.
The beauty in destruction is not to forget.
We all deserve paradise for the world we live
in.

Weakness comes when adrenaline fails.
With Solitude, desperation lives.
Decisions and character flails.
When reputation is threatened, aggression
gives.

Searching for existence that isn't clear.
Like certain things I believe are real.
The Devil and myself.
The thunder and the rain.
The sun, the moon;

regret and pain.

Advice is useless when the lesson isn't there.
A heart is destructive when it doesn't feel.

SOLITUDE AND GRATITUDE

Sometimes I dream so much it creates pain.
I understand the bitterness of the rich that
forever remains.
Ungrateful pleasures in life aren't just;
like the shine of metal erodes to rust.

Gratitude of tongues never meant so much.
Success means nothing if you yourself are not
touched.
Solidarity creates fuel for the mind;
like Adversity and hate have done for mankind.

I no longer want to do for others what I can't do
for myself.
Those that want from me, must do themselves.
I wish the train I dream about would take me to
the destination.
Where a lonely tent overlooking the sea awaits
my meditation.

My motivation to thrive every day is a
testament to my fatigue and reason.
For the sleep I crave creates dreams of regret,
solitude and prison.

The respect that follows me only falsifies my
moderation in life.

The sleep that I enjoy, and the breaths I take are
often in strife.

My dreams are numbered, and the countdown
remains.
With every gamble there's the reminder the
debt comes due someday.
Crossroads in life begin when regrets ail,
the weakness comes when adrenaline fails.

AWAKENING

Every day I awake in belief I'm among the
living,
but every ceasing convulsion equals an actual
nightmare.
Maybe I can stay asleep long enough to forget
the day?
How to feel alive and happy?
I can't remember.

Instead, my being uncovers actuality in tremors.
I can't shake what I can't control.
I examine fact, fiction and what makes sense
what is needed to keep breathing.

Rations don't hold when the rain keeps coming.

I'm Hoping I can survive the day without
hunger reminding me of need.
Happiness only forms from good memories.
It reminds me that friendship only comes
momentarily.

Rain cleanses the soul, but the sun dries out the
troubles.
The only hope in a troubled soul are the clouds
that shadow the shame.
The heart doesn't win in a shallow world.
Only the desperation that results in fooling the
kind.

Legends are only good when the dumb are
innocent.
The victor is spoiled when the fans expect
honesty forever.
When the skin is no longer tight,
and when the motives are no longer right;
the sudden instinct is dead.

The spring is lost when the weak before, have
gone lame.
The mind has gone soft in a world that doesn't
explain.
No morals surpass when many have felt pain.

When pride has finally been beaten
and your confidence is no longer respected,
there's no hope for stature, and no reason for
trying.

BECOMING

Where a place takes you back in time to the
Perfect scenery.
Invisible like ghosts in the fog brush past the
statue you created within yourself.
It's the same depiction as searching for where
you are going and remembering where you
been.

When the search for others to fill a void takes
you nowhere;
you take the solo path to what makes you
better, and always will.

I control the demons within me.

Beautiful Sunday massacres always reflect the
evenings past.
Daunting side shows from the unconscious
mind bring inconsistent tragedies that never
equal common certainties.

I control the demons within me.

Virtues take flight to warranted excuses,
as kind gestures block out a twisted soul.
Evil ruptures a bleeding passion,
signifying constant functional tendencies.
Sunrise mornings awake a loathing grudge.

I control the demons within me.

Never- ending idealistic fears flush out
pulsating nearsighted dreams.
Wretched hands from holding horrific
memories,
from the broken arms of an old clock;
comes the time for the bleeding to stop.
Others before yourself bring inconsistent
determinations.

I control the demons within me.

Others before yourself bring inconsistent
determinations.
I control the demons within me.
Others before yourself bring inconsistent
determinations.

BECOMING II

The difference between life and death when
you are at the lowest point of your story,
is finding the ambition and motivation to
realize that your time of triumph is ahead.
Most can't fathom the fact that we are actually
our strongest when we are at rock bottom.
I have always believed it is life's test for us to
dig deep down inside; find the talents we have
and use those as our reasons to survive and
succeed.
In many ways it has saved my life.

The difference between the rich and the poor
are simply ideas.

CHARACTER

Your character is more than what you stand for
and how you live your life.
More importantly, it's who you keep in your
inner circle.
Reflection and the realization of the man that
you are
comes from who you had in your circle and
what their character was.
Nothing should make you feel weaker than
realizing you had cowardly men and woman
rather than stand up people in your life.
Friendship is a fog and respect is cheap when
there are people who give it to low lives.

THE DREAM

It was as if I were back in that same cage again.
Giving it everything I had to prove I was as
tough as they said I was.
Every drop of sweat matched every breath I
chased.
Though I knocked out every man before,
no matter what I threw at him he wouldn't go
down.

Sometimes the hardest punches you throw in
life will still leave your opponent standing.
The important thing is that you face challenges.
No matter how tough or how unrealistic they
may seem;
finish them with no regrets.
There is no defeat within fearlessness.

GRANDUER

I distance myself because I want to keep that
persona.
The one I have given to so many in my life.
I don't ever want to disappoint those that
believe what they do about me.
I care about too many to ever let them inside.
Inside allows the option to change their mind.
I try and make lasting impressions onto
everyone I meet.
Without great intentions or amazing grandeur,
but unexpectantly through imperfections and
complexity.
A mysterious nature protects unraveled hearts
so diligently.

INTERNAL INDEBTNESS

We all want to be so much in life,
and for some we end up wanting to be too
much.
The problems begin when the achievements just
aren't enough.
When we seem to have done everything we
have ever wanted to do.
Moving forward, we face the days where there
is nothing left to do
but live the rest of our lives understanding the
reasons,
and learning to live with the demons that kept
us motivated to live a life that simply wasn't
ours to begin with.
We can fail doing what simply doesn't make us
happy
so, why not take a chance in failing doing what
we love?
Happiness is only an illusion;
we all suffer under the reign of a smile.
Do what reminds you that you have a soul and
build a life around that.

INTRINSIC TEARS

There's not a better intrinsic honor then
watching the eyes of the faithful fill with tears.
Respecting me as a person and what I've meant
too them for years.

How is it I can be blessed with admiration from so many?
Why have I reached the masses, and why does love come to me so easy?
It's this that reminds me that this heart of mine still ticks with passion.
Unable to imagine the sorrow of not knowing virtue through possession.
I can't stomach those that have nothing but stagnation in their souls.
The weak, the weary and those that live pulseless waiting to turn old.
We shall not want only through what's right, but take to our hearts what forever lives in our mind.

HEARTS CADEANCE

I'm a man and I'm to love.
I'll always attract those that will never leave.
Years before and years to come;
they'll always be right here for me.

With this beautiful curse I must pay
a price for those that damaged my soul.
Although the wreckage; I'd rather love this way.
To keep the fire burning, so interests never slow.

The secret to passion is conversation.

It builds within hearts and minds.
Deep and meaningful talk is mesmerizing.
The connection through talk will never unwind.

Memories and feelings always seem to fade.
When the loneliness begins though,
your heart beats a familiar echo;
to the true love of a person who is never
forgotten or betrayed.

Lust is indebted to who you truly respect and
owe.
I have loved more than authors have storied.
I'll never regret the hearts I have taken,
and I'll never forget the closeness we have
shared.
Our intimacy always shook this foundation.

Your thoughts are my thoughts always.
Your heart will always beat in cadence with
mine;
for as long as this outer circle spins this way,
the end of our desires has no time.

IF I COULD FLY

If I could only fly;
I could be as big as the dreams that push me.
I could see the passions that lift me.
If I could only fly;

I could see the love that surrounds me,
and recognize the needs that replenish me.
If we could only fly;
we could see the world is empty,
without a reason to fulfill it.

SONGS

JON

Your heart was always tearing, but you can't
weep.
The pain was always sickening, but you won't
speak.
How'd you pick your rope?
What's the last words that you wrote?
How'd you smoke your dope?

You lost your mother's comfort.
Now you can't trust.
Walls are always crumbling.
Now you just wish.

You watch your children growing,
the pain was always showing.
Why'd you give them up?

You're so alone.
You can't feel the hope.
You can't shake the urge.
You can't turn back time.
You can't hide the pain when the dark remains.
When the need is gone so is the quest for life.
You can't cry and you can't feel.

Kindness made for something, but you can't
win.
Life respects the suffering; your peace is now
our pain.
You should have been here together,
but you died in the same manner.
The hemorrhage in my blood.

You're so alone.
You can't feel the hope.
You can't shake the urge.
You can't turn back time.
You can't hide the pain when the dark remains.
When the need is gone so is the quest for life.
You can't cry and you can't feel.

How'd you pick your rope?
What's the last words that you wrote?
Did you wear your shoes?

DEMON'S TERROR

I walk across that fire to hang my cross to bear.
Just to feel his hands upon me,
but you can't shake what demons' terror.
I try to close my eyes because it's easier to see,

but the devil's minds beside me while I lay
down and try.
Regrets and my sorrows begin with the sunset.
Insomnia overcomes me.
A lesson learned through death.
I don't know where to go,
I don't know what to know.
My demons are running wild,
but as long as I'm doing fine.
I don't know when to love,
I don't know when to love.
Your heart was always full of lies.

MY GIRL

(Lyrics by Joe Trader Music by Jason Amerson)

When we met, my eyes were captured.
My Attention expanded; my mind was tortured.
Now when you talk, I try to listen.
It's not that I don't care.
I just don't know what to say.

My girl, can you see?
My girl, can you feel me?
When we talk, we don't speak.
My girl, can you hear me?

When you're gone, I try to live.
I lie.
These demons reign.
Now when I walk, I walk alone.
It's not that I don't try.
I just don't know what to give.

My girl, can you see?
My girl, can you feel me?
When we talk, we don't speak.
My girl, can you hear me?

THE NEED TO WEEP

We walk along through the tall flowers.
And then we fall when the demons shower.
Who are We to bleed?
I told you I'm a virgin.
Leave a rose for the broken.
I feel the urge to weep.

But there's too much love to give to only one
person.
I want you on your knees, Because I yearn for
affection.
Love is all I need; but I settled for addiction.
I live with broken mirrors.

I can't handle the reflection.

We're coming home from the wars and their
taking our babies.
But, what for?
I'll trade her for my scars.

I need you by my side.
I'm only one person.
I tried living life alone, but you're a better
version.

You got me on my knees.
Our hearts beat in cadence.
Give all your fears to me.
Your infectious and I need it.

I give my heart to bleed.
I want you on your knees.
I'm begging darling please.
I'll be your everything.
Give all your fears to me.

LOVE IS LOST

I tend to leave so much that it creates the pain.
It's hard to keep the lust when the failure
remains.
Virtues in life are never enough.

Love means nothing if it's not you that's
touched.

The words you needed were never enough.
So, you walked away when times got rough.
You wasted your life searching for love,
but in the end, you never knew what it was.

The loneliness comes when the instincts fail.
X2

Love is lost when confidence fails. X3

"Without tragedy there are no demons, and without demons there are no beautiful creations."

REFLECTIONS

"Time was meant to comprehend reasons to forget the past, the reasons to learn, remember and progress. Without the ability to understand reflection, we will never gain perfection."

MOTIVATION

"Perseverance is the internal flame that stays ignited through the roadblocks of life. It's about staying motivated to keep going no matter how far the goal may be and how hard it is going to be in order to achieve it." Joe Trader – The Purpose – Living Journal

- We are all authors in this world, not just the character in this book of life. Script your own chapters for the life you want for yourself. Only you have the pen. Keep writing forward, and remember your story is not finished yet

- The greatest human challenge is motivation. With motivation one can become anything. Without the challenge to find motivation within yourself; one will only remain average.

- Everyone has their own agenda to your master plan once it's almost finished, but only one person has the brilliance to make it a reality. Not everyone fits the mold. You can call me cocky or stubborn, I don't care. I have never understood the point of giving anyone else credit for your accomplishments. Nobody force fed you the motivation you needed to become a champion or successful in life. You did it. I'm sorry that I pity those that try and jump on the band wagon that they tried but failed to construct in the past. You had the tools but couldn't construct it without a teacher.

- One of the greatest things about life is there is never an expiration date on achievement.
- The best investment you can make in life is in yourself.
- The only advantage we have in life is staying positive.
- Be wise in your new endeavors but wiser trusting individuals that come from behind to pat your back. Remember your only investment and trust your only friend. Yourself.
- A weak man can easily break the rules ineffectively, but only a strong man can break the rules and make his own successfully.
- We all have those dreams but procrastinate on when to begin the process. The motivated ones don't sit around and wait for a prefect time. Champions create that perfect time and the greatest figures are those who create leaders in the process.
- Hustle Is LIFE.
- Life is filled with critics and doubters. The greatest advantage over them is yourself and the fact that you can prove them wrong. Don't let negativity defeat true talent.

- Never allow others to judge you by your weakness, instead let them hate you for your greatness.
- Unfortunate experiences in life are only negative if you choose to not benefit and learn from them. You can turn anything into a positive. You can always beat the odds.
- The way you address life and handle the pressures, success and failures is going to mold you into the person you will be remembered as. Nobody who chose the easy road and nobody who lived the average life is ever remembered, and one thing is for certain; you sure as hell don't need friends to reach the top.
- We are all authors in this world, not just the character in this book of life. Script your own chapters for the biography you want for yourself. Only you have the pen. Keep writing forward, and remember your story is not finished yet.
- Any bad experience in life is needed. For more than realizing how blessed we are, but rather to understand that blessings constitute respect, appreciation and the investment in talent.
- Complications only enable one's mind to expand beyond what it's accustomed to; equaling a better understanding, an inner

intrinsic reward, and accomplishing the greatest possible decision.

- If there's nothing worth fighting for, there's nothing worth living for.
- Life is filled with critics and doubters. The biggest advantage to them is you, and the fact that you can prove them wrong.
- Having the will to succeed reflects your purpose behind the idea, and passion sustains the why in the reason. This is how motivation is born.
- One of the biggest insults to yourself, is continuing to let that voice inside remind you what you should be doing to better yourself without acting.
- Search for the gold, work for the goal, hope for the best but expect the worst. That way emotionally you will never be beaten. Prepare for your next mission despite defeat. That way you can never lose
- What stands in front of your goals? What do you have to do to be clear about it? You have the power to achieve anything.
- You will never be the person you want to be if pressure, stress and discipline are taken out of your life.

- Pure talent will get you remembered but dedication will make you unforgettable.
- One of the most rewarding things you can do in life is letting go of what you thought was real.
- Your thoughts, your words and your actions are the only things in life you can control. If you live your life believing you can control anything else, you will be struggling in life forever.
- Life is all about time, human nature and who throws the most jabs. The victory, however, comes from those who have the bigger hands.
- One good idea a day can be the difference between a mediocre future, and success.
- Find the things that make you happy and gain from them.
- If there is one thing, I have truly come to believe the last year as I continue to construct this unique business of mine; it's this. I have lost all faith in the reliability of man. If you wait around for others to help you, you will never get to where you want to be in life. You have family at best, expect nothing from anyone and always remain that person everyone can trust. More importantly, trust yourself.
- It's what's in your head that determines what's in your hands.

- It's not about what a man believes, it's what he does.
- The greatest instinctive motives come from battered will.
- In order to benefit the greatest from an overwhelming success, one must thicken their efforts into minimal advancements.
- Motivation is a better investment than education.
- It's better to fail with imagination then succeed with originality.
- Only advantage we have in life is staying positive.
- It doesn't really matter what a person's intentions are or even what they believe. Only your actions make you the person you will be remembered as.
- I'm in no hurry for possibilities, but I'm always hustling for opportunities
- I don't have time to take my time.
- Great leaders don't create followers, they create other leaders. Even if they don't, they never needed the help anyways. I envy those that did it on their own. Those who refused to trust anyone and wore frowns in the process. The ones that risked what little they had in order to gain the unknown, and the Americans that are

not scared to stand up to a system that stand to oppress.

- Those that walk around with a fuck you attitude because they know the secret to success are my hero's. The main goal in everybody's life should be simple. Realize the problem, be a part of change and spend what time you have proving others wrong.
- It's never too late to start an empire, and you're never too old to chase a dream. There are many sunrises left to begin a new journey, and plenty of sunsets left to remind you of what you forgot to do in your life.
- Great Ideas amongst turmoil equals a brilliant mind.
- In your greatest moments of disappointment is where you find out who you are. Motivated or defeated?
- I don't hold onto the past. I invest in it.
- Self-motivation is self-contagious.
- When it rains it pours, but nobody has ever been able to change the weather except time and patience so, I will never pretend I can. Instead, I will wait it out and determine the reasons the rain was needed.
- Life is a rehearsal, but your performance is real.

COURAGE AND PERSERVERANCE

"Courage derives from many things. It's not just putting your life in danger but rather putting yourself in front of an obstacle that you know has an advantage against you." Joe Trader – The Purpose – Living Journal

- Logics represent reality.
- Advice. Just another wasted effort.
- Living this life one bedroom at a time still don't draw windows.
- Never let what you once were define you. Let it refine you.
- Life has tolerance for strong people who can tolerate life.
- Nobody escapes this life without making a mistake or two. If you find a way to become a better person from them, you'll live with no regrets.
- We are all impatient. Having patience through impatience is what equals success.
- Most of us don't get to choose the road we are put on in life. For some of us the road is rough, uneven and altered by washouts from the rain that often comes into our lives. We can't

predict the weather that changes our paths, but we can choose to either grade over the divots that continue to occur from the storms or decide to pave the way for a smoother ride to our destination.

- There's no better accomplishment then knowing as you close your eyes to sleep there's others out there that can't sleep because of you.
- Turn Frustrations into Ideas.
- To be a champion, one must know the difference between fact and truth. Fact is reality, and truth is our perception of reality. Create your reality. If your dreams don't scare you, they aren't big enough.
- A voice will reach multitudes, but actions will affect masses.
- Embrace the mystery of life and that you are at your strongest point mentally in the moments of disparity. This is life's test to use your strengths and your best qualities to make the best out of the situation for yourself and to help others.

VISION

"With faith and hope, you can get through anything, no matter how bad it seems." Joe Trader – The Purpose – Living Journal

- You can't judge a book by its cover or even the story that's in it. It's what you get out of the story that matters; not what's in it.
- We must not develop within ourselves what others want us to reflect but create from within what purpose we want to affect.
- Scars are decoration, not ugliness.
- They say you shouldn't judge a book by its cover, but you sure the hell can judge the preference to determine whether it's worth reading.
- Choose your worries wisely.
- A moment of clarity is the best remedy to a lifetime of pain.
- Education has taught me how to think, but education has not taught me how to live. It's the trenches of reality that has shown me the beast of life and given me the tools to survive. The key to life is live.
- Leadership is not inherited, it is developed and learned. Dedication beats talent, and karma is a bitch.
- Goals should never be something of the past. They should become addictive.
- I don't think holding onto the past is normal, but I think remembering the past is crucial.

- I never understood why people fear hate. Anger is a gift if you can use it strategically. It's true commitment. To love is too easy. That's why we all hurt, and that's why the world is so fragile and weak.
- We all have demons. It's what makes the world interesting.
- An occasional act will never equal a Constant attitude.
- Human nature is best when it's at its worst.
- The past is the past. You're defined by it unless you symbolize your future.
- Those that tend to show hate towards others only proves hate for themselves. It makes them feel better about what's missing in their own life.
- Sometimes we see the invaluable as valuable before we see the value in what really matters.
- If I was stronger, I could carry this world. If I had no intentions I would escape. Every day is better than yesterday.
- You can be anything you want in life, but you can't be everything.
- Life's always about having to leave, but you're always going somewhere.
- Pay attention to the men who many know but have few friends. Pay attention to what they

have in common and what they have accomplished; then pay closer attention to the reward.

- You can either break the wind or become the storm that comes with it.
- I think it's ignorant when people say you shouldn't judge a book by its cover. Sometimes the cover is exactly a reflection of what the book entails. You better read the forward very carefully before you begin the first chapter.
- Never stay with someone because you feel like they need your support
  and never spend the relationship giving that person confidence they will never have on their own.
- A talented mind equals constant creative turmoil. Those good times will never return, and old age can't commit to its downfall.
  Within these hands erupts memories of youth.
  Its tragedy won't submit to what's ahead.
  The pulse just can't beat to time, and the heart has no remorse to age.
  With the mind to breed there's no blood to fill the need. What more do we have to give?
- Nothing should make you feel weaker than realizing you had cowardly men rather than stand up guys in your crew. Friendship is a fog and respect is cheap when there are people who give it to low lives.

- You don't need to look very far to find someone that will make you feel better about your own nightmare.
- Sometimes happens all the time, but regret doesn't have to.
- There's not a better feeling in the world than knowing as I lay my head down tonight kings are losing sleep knowing I'm headed in their direction.
- I rarely remember all the things I've said, but at least I forget only some of the things I remember.
- **Our style curtails our vision and our sacred imagination which can never be explained. It's only virtue that constructs our passions into beautiful fixtures.**
- Never let your instincts be overshadowed by guilt. You'll look like a fool.
- Happiness is best when consumed momentarily; not continually or expectantly.
- We are born alone, and we die alone. Where we grow in between is where we learn. What and who matters most in our life is ourselves. It's there which we capture the meaning of the beginning and the end of existence. We are what matters, we are the only one we truly know, and we are the only soul we can trust.
- Whoever came up with the phrase "Money can't buy you happiness." is a fool and obviously has never experienced being broke and living in

poverty. You may have riches elsewhere with health, a great family, friends, a glamorous body and multitudes of gorgeous dates, but nothing beats money, and nothing makes you happier. Nothing.

- Sadness is the end to something good and depression is feeling like there is nothing good to a beginning.
- Life never slows down, and life is never afraid to force drastic changes that force us to adapt. Why do we tend to think it's ok to slow down with age, and why are we afraid to make a drastic change in order to better our own lives?
- You can own cars, a fancy home, a beautiful stature and plenty of bright ideas that force feed motivation. The greatest investment I have found in my life are simply those days where I am given the peace of mind of not having to worry about struggle.
- The best thing about getting older is how easy it becomes to dismiss those with no regard to loyalty out of your life.
I wish I knew then what I know now. I could have been happier earlier.
- The everyday battle of actual challenge is something every man dreams of, but only the greatest are willing to endure the pain it takes to accomplish greatness.
- Contrary to popular believe; all people are not created equal, nor will we ever see the day we

will be treated like it. This is America. We rule by class. Look around you.

- We are all perfect at first.
- You can't force yourself to love someone, and when you try you will only hurt yourself. The impossible control is the feeling of loneliness, and the thought of stability. The secret though, is not allowing yourself to believe you loved someone or you need someone because of those feelings. Never let your gut feelings be overshadowed by guilt. You will end up looking like a fool.
- The biggest sign of weakness is in your posts. You cry to a crowd of people that only 1% care to read and that's if you're lucky. Your narcissism believes however, that everyone cares. The proof of being naive to your own false pretenses is the fact that the ones you supposedly need and who are there, you don't take their advice anyways. Therefore, you really are your biggest fan, and you are indeed your biggest enemy.
- Excuses hide what we fear.
- I never understood why people worry about lost paths in their lives. I have always thought that being lost is a key factor in molding who you are. Continuous progression, always moving forward, learning from your surroundings,

options, alternatives and remembering wrong turns is crucial. Being lost is never the place you want to be, but it's the only way we get to where we contently belong. Never knowing where you belong should only motivate you to better your routes in life, and never stop learning. Never settle and Embrace your struggles.

- Relationships and communication are dead because we are really only interested in ourselves. We realize just how lonely the world actually is when we are not scrolling through social media, and the days of escaping because you need time alone without Facebook putting out a search party for you is gone. No wonder we are lost.

- The easiest thing for some is being physically attractive. The most challenging thing for most is staying humble about it.

- When I evaluate my goals and my plans to accomplish them, I always remember the importance of patience. Timing is everything in life, and control of development is often defiant to the demands of life. When you are frustrated because things are not going as planned, take a moment and recognize the lessons in traffic. What's the point of being in a hurry when there is just a red light waiting for you?

- Your happiness should not have to be compromised to modify the happiness for others.
- I speak for all single men and woman when I say new pets can ruin the mood more than old exes.
- Talk is the easiest form of expression, but communication is the most complicated of arts. Feeling's, however, must be able to control the outcomes of emotion for the proper comprehensions for success.
- Always so gorgeous, confident and irresistible in your selfies. The most evident reflection, however, is you're also always so alone and single in them too.
- Keep being you and expect only good things from yourself. Be nice to others without asking for anything in return so you will never be disappointed. The greatest thing you can hope will find you, is someone who holds the same philosophy.
- Respect is unforgiving.
  Honor is unforgettable.
  Trust is unmerciful.
  Love is hypocritical.
  Loyalty is timeless.
  Victory is contagious.
  Defeat is enshrined.

Jealously is earned.
- Happiness is often mistaken by the fuse of angry confidence.
- Rain can't soak what is not there, will can't always shake what demon's terror, karma can't always afford happiness to those that seek it, and great fortune doesn't exist just because you receive it.
- Lonesome is simply popularity turned inside out.
- Strong people accept what they are given when they have given their all.
- The secret to healing within this life so we may again experience the success and happiness we deserve, is finding the good within the bad.
- If there is one thing, I have learned in life it is that respect, loyalty, compassion and maturity will confront your true character.
  How do you get over someone's lack of respect and compassion? By looking at that person's character and the respect that has outlined their entire life.
  Disrespect should be respected when it comes from someone who is respected, not someone who's only friend is materialism and envy.
  If they have nothing, they are nothing.
  Compassion for the compassionless is the definition of foolishness.

- What will you do when you're old and your beauty is no longer your best attribute or your best excuse to why you deserve more than what you have? Only a desperate man invests in beauty alone, and only a woman who lacks confidence believes it's all that's needed to be taken care of.

PASSION

- Crazy doesn't need a reason because all madmen have a purpose. It's where passion comes from.
- I'm not here in this life to be a fixture in any one thing. I'm here to be a defining moment in people's lives for many reasons. That's what success means to me.
- Take advantage of every opportunity to be happy, even if it's only for a moment. You never know when you'll need it later in life.
- Leadership and advice go hand in hand. The right advice is easy to take, and anyone can be a leader. Without the passion and motivation to find the truth in either, they often become a wasted talent.
- It's not what the world offers you that may offer peace, but rather what you offer the world that may grant you peace from within.

- The thought of compassion always overshadows reality when reality becomes your penance.
- Turn the worst possible outcome into the best possible opportunity.
- "What am I doing for someone else today?" Should always be a question on your agenda.
- In order to benefit the greatest from an overwhelming success, one must thicken their efforts into minimal advancements.
- Take advantage of every opportunity to be happy even if it's only for a moment, even though it may not be morally correct and even though you know it may hurt you in the end. You never know when you'll need those memories later in life.
- While haters hate, creators create.
- The most sick and twisted thing about life is it is designed to beat you to the ground. The most hypocritical thing about love is often it results in hate, and the most ruthless thing about fate is that it punishes you for trying to better yourself and the lives of others. Although I understand and often envy those that give up instead of fighting; the disease of pride simply won't allow me too.

PURPOSE

"I just know that when I am an old man, I want to look back on my life and say I used my body and mind to their max, because I believe it is a shame to waste it." Joe Trader – The Purpose – Living Journal

- Any bad experience in life is needed. For more than realizing how blessed we are, but rather to understand that blessings constitute respect, appreciation and the investment in talent.
- The key to life is live everyday as an option. The option to succeed, the option to progress, the option to learn or the option to fail. Don't let the option of regret burden you. Your talents depend on you.
- There's nothing funny about a man who says he has a dream. It's only funny when they spend their entire lives talking about it, never

achieving it because their mouth was always worth more than their mind.

- I have no remorse or patience for those who show up late, lack motivation or work ethic, and live an average life, but I understand it. God, do I envy you for not giving a shit because I sure the hell could never get to that level.

- Effort can't always change what's meant to be in a story. Sometimes the most important part of the book is in the epilogue where it reads "I tried."

- We only have one experience in this world and life sure as hell isn't fair or perfect so, nobody expects you to be either. The only way we can get even from our imperfections is by simply helping others.

- Sometimes it's hard to know exactly which lane to be in on a two-way road of life. Especially knowing the times make the man but the man can also make the times. If your headed in right direction, we should be blessed we have those choices. No matter what exit you take, it's never too late to get to where you want to be in life.

- Sometimes believing in something you can't see makes more sense than believing in something right in front of you.

- You can create anything you want in life, but you will never be able to fill an incurable void in your life. All we can do is the best that we can with the passions we have, and hope we leave an impression.
- The greatest enemy to your legacy is going to bed dreaming you're something better than the life you'll live tomorrow.
- I prefer to date dreams and goals. Accomplishments never break your heart.
- Our biggest victories in life don't often come with recognition or rewards, but instead the lessons that are learned through experience and the person we become through character.
- Those who do not dream withhold because they believe they have nothing to offer the world. Champions know that confidence, like intimacy is infinite. There is no end until their hearts stop beating.
- Being hated and ridiculed out of shear ignorance is simply respect and grandeur turned inside out. To remain immune to that nature and victorious; one must produce resilience.
- If you don't wake up every day with a goal in mind, and something worth your best efforts; your simply not living.
- When deep breaths no longer hold in the anger, it's time to make the biggest decision in your life.

- Distinction is categorically characterized.
- Everyday people wake up, look in the mirror and tell themselves they are going to change their life and never do. Change comes from opportunity and benefiting from an opportunity means leaving the past, and those who remained stagnant in your life behind you. Nobody sympathizes with those with weak friends and relentless omissions.
- How life can change in an instant and redirect all that was once forward. If only for a small fraction of that path takes your eyes off what lied ahead, let that new view change your focus into a brighter future when you look back ahead.
- In times of trouble, your greatest strategy for triumph is within.
- Don't think about the discretionary of the past. They won't make you any better than yesterday.
- The past is the past. You're only defined by it unless you symbolize your future
- Live life like karma's chasing you.
  (A quote which became a tattoo for a fan)
- There is a bit of greatness in everyone, but within that greatness often signifies the toughest ideas. The greatest tragedy one can do to themselves is allow a great idea to burden

their mind and never act upon it. Here's to all those great ideas that we never saw and here's to the people whose ideas keep them up at night. Don't waste them, embrace them.

- There's the reality of who you are and There's the vision of what you want to be. Whether or not you except these choices, and if you are not careful, you may die as one and take to your grave what you never became. The underlining factor in your life is finding the passion for who you should be.

- We all have a story. It's what we do with it, how we tell it and whether we can motivate others through it that creates a lesson.

- We all have a past. It's what we do today that matters, not what we left behind.

- All we have are the choices we make. With that, the choice to learn and progress, or forever be burdened by the outcome you could have embraced with possibility.

- The most successful individuals and the greatest leaders remember imperious situations.

- How can you expect life to do right in you when you continue to do wrong in life?

- I don't believe in bad luck. I believe that life gets even, I believe for each heart you break you pay a price, and I believe the only way you win the battles we face every day is to never except that things are the way they are just because life says so.

- To some, life's all about simple existence, but simple won't grant you success.
- All we have in the end is our efforts. Not exactly what we left behind, but what we tried to accomplish and the fortitude we used as the blueprint to the possibility. The investment in time, opportunity or the careen it took to be noticed is insignificant, but instead the magnitude in which we left the impression.
- I don't have much here as far as luxury goes. I suppose what one sees as luxury I see as a reflection of condition. Luxuries to me are simply being able to live your life free of the burdens of worry.
- As you step out the door this morning, remember we are all authors in this world, not just the character in this book of life. Script your own chapters for the biography you want for yourself. Only you have the pen. Keep writing forward. And remember your story is not finished yet.
- To live spiritually minded one must recognize that some of the worries in our lives come from our own sins. We can live in regret or answer the call that asks us to help others through those

same burdens. That's how being forgiven is done.

- Just remember, that those that tend to show hate towards you only proves hate for themselves. It makes them feel better to criticize you in order to feel better about what's missing in their own life. Therefore, keep being you.

For:

My Grandma Rose, who supposedly wrote a book, but was gone before she had the chance to finish it.
A writer, musician, educator, biblical scholar and an Army Veteran. A survivor of life's toughest lessons. I see more of you in myself the older I get.

My Daughter Grace. My greatest love and motivation in life. May you always remember those three lessons I taught you early on. Never Give up, always work hard, and never be scared.
I hope someday you will recognize how much you impacted me, and how you impacted thousands through my work and love for you. Even more important, is that you understand how hard I worked to be more of a father to you.

FEATURES AND RECOMONDATIONS

Badger Tough
Bennington Wrestling: A Tradition of
Excellence
By Craig Sesker

The Purpose - Living Journal
Influence That Inspires Integrity
By Paul E. Bryant

Purpose Living Leader
By Paul E. Bryant